WORLD LEADERS

EMMANUEL MACRON
PRESIDENT OF FRANCE

by Rebecca Rowell

FOCUS READERS

www.focusreaders.com

Focus Readers is distributed by North Star Editions:
sales@northstareditions.com | 888-417-0195

Produced for Focus Readers by Red Line Editorial.

Content Consultant: Alice Conklin, Professor of History, Ohio State University

Photographs ©: Christophe Ena/AP Images, cover, 1; Jerome Mars/Sipa/AP Images, 4–5; Guillaume Destombes/Shutterstock Images, 7; EQRoy/Shutterstock Images, 8–9, 20–21; LaMiaFotografia/Shutterstock Images, 11; lynea/Shutterstock Images, 12–13; Guillaume Louyot Onickz Artworks/Shutterstock Images, 15; Regis Duvignau/Reuters/AP Images, 17; Anatoly Tiplyashin/Shutterstock Images, 19; Frederic Legrand - Comeo/Shutterstock Images, 23, 25; Eliot Blondet/Sipa/AP Images, 26–27; Hadrian/Shutterstock Images, 29; Laurent Cipriani/AP Images, 31; Villard/Sipa/AP Images, 32–33; Red Line Editorial, 35, 43; Thanassis Stavrakis/AP Images, 37; Francois Mori/AP Images, 39; Villard-Witt/Sipa/AP Images, 40–41; Etienne Laurent/AP Images, 45

ISBN
978-1-63517-548-6 (hardcover)
978-1-63517-620-9 (paperback)
978-1-63517-764-0 (ebook pdf)
978-1-63517-692-6 (hosted ebook)

Library of Congress Control Number: 2017948132

Printed in the United States of America
Mankato, MN
November, 2017

ABOUT THE AUTHOR
Rebecca Rowell has put her degree in publishing and writing to work as an editor and author, working on dozens of books. Recent topics as an author include environmentalists Rachel Carson and Sylvia Earle. She lives in Minneapolis, Minnesota.

TABLE OF CONTENTS

CHAPTER 1

MACRON GETS HIS WISH

In 2016, Emmanuel Macron was part of the French government. But he wasn't a politician. He was minister of the economy. His job was to advise the nation's president, François Hollande, on money matters. Macron had many ideas to boost the country's economy. But Hollande wouldn't put them into place. Macron would need to take a different approach. So he started his own political party, quit his job, and ran for president.

Emmanuel Macron worked in the Ministry of the Economy, also known as Bercy.

In April 2017, voters cast their ballots in the first round of the presidential election. The two candidates with the most votes would move on to the final round. Macron came in first, with nearly 24 percent. Marine Le Pen was a close second.

Macron was an **independent** and a **centrist**. He wanted to unite the French people. He also wanted to improve France's relationship with the European Union (EU). This is a group of European nations that work together on shared issues.

Many French citizens were divided over high unemployment and immigration. Recent **terror** attacks had scared the nation. Some citizens thought stricter immigration laws would prevent future attacks. They hoped limits on immigration would also create jobs for the French people.

Le Pen represented the National Front, a party that promotes **nationalism**. Unlike Macron, Le Pen

▲ The race between Macron and Marine Le Pen caused a divide between French voters.

was an experienced politician. She had placed third in the 2012 presidential election. Le Pen wanted France to leave the EU. She also wanted to limit the number of immigrants entering France.

On May 7, 2017, voters made their choice. Macron won 66 percent of the votes. He easily defeated Le Pen. A week later, he took office as president of France. At 39 years old, he became the youngest president in French history.

CHAPTER 2

LIFE BEFORE POLITICS

Emmanuel Macron was born in Amiens, France, in 1977. He was the first of three children. His parents and siblings are all doctors. He was the only one in his family who didn't go into medicine.

Emmanuel studied science in high school. But when he went to college, he changed his focus. He studied public service at the Paris Institute of Political Sciences, or Sciences Po. In 2001, he earned a graduate degree in **public policy**.

According to one of his teachers at Sciences Po, Emmanuel often led class debates.

He also studied philosophy at Paris Nanterre University. During his studies, he worked for the famous French philosopher Paul Ricœur.

Next, Macron attended the École Nationale d'Administration (ENA), or National School of Administration. Many ENA students go on to hold top positions in government and business. Macron graduated from the ENA in 2004.

Macron took his first government job that same year. He worked as a finance inspector in the French Ministry of Economy. But in 2008, Macron decided to leave public service. He wanted to work in private business instead.

Macron began working for a French bank. He advised the international food company Nestlé. Macron helped Nestlé buy part of a company called Pfizer. The deal cost Nestlé nearly $12 billion. Macron's success with Nestlé helped

 Several French presidents have attended the National School of Administration.

him build a positive reputation. Many French politicians wanted him as their financial adviser. The attention was an important stepping-stone in Macron's path to the presidency.

CHAPTER 3

A BRIEF INTRODUCTION TO FRANCE

The nation that Macron now leads has a long history. In fact, France is one of the oldest nations in the world. For centuries, the nation was a monarchy. This meant it was ruled by a king and queen. Then in 1792, the country briefly became a **republic**. During the 1800s and 1900s, the country had various governments. Leadership alternated between monarchies and republics.

Marie Antoinette was the last queen of France before the First Republic.

Today, France is in the Fifth Republic, which began in 1958.

France has three branches of government. The legislative branch is in charge of making laws. It consists of a parliament with two houses, the National Assembly and the Senate. The National Assembly has 577 seats, and the Senate has 348 seats. Citizens elect members of the National Assembly. Mayors and other elected officials choose members of the Senate. Each house reviews laws proposed by either the prime minister (PM) or a Parliament member. Bills must be approved by both houses to become laws.

> ## ➤ THINK ABOUT IT

What other countries can you think of that have or have had a monarchy? What other countries are republics?

▲ The National Assembly meets in the Palais Bourbon, which dates back to the 1700s.

The judicial branch includes the Court of Cassation, the highest court in France. The Court of Cassation has a variety of judges, including 120 trial judges. The president appoints the judges. The judicial system includes lower-level courts as well, including regional courts.

The executive branch includes the president and the PM. The president is the head of the government and represents the nation in **foreign affairs**. French voters elect the president in two rounds of voting. This is how Macron became president in 2017. The president serves a five-year term and may be elected to a second term.

According to France's constitution, the PM directs government actions. The president appoints the PM. The president also appoints members of the cabinet, known as the Council of Ministers. Ministers oversee a variety of areas, including culture, the environment, and national security.

On May 17, 2017, Macron named Édouard Philippe as the PM. Macron also appointed 22 ministers. Half of these ministers were women. A gender-equal cabinet was one of Macron's

▲ In 2012, François Hollande (second from right) assigned France's first gender-equal cabinet.

campaign promises. As of 2017, the French cabinet was one of only six in the world without a male majority.

France has more than a dozen political parties. In June 2017, candidates from Macron's party won a majority in the National Assembly. Many observers expected this to help Macron push items through the legislative branch.

FOCUS ON
FRANCE

France's capital, Paris, is known for its culture and cuisine. The city is home to 11 million residents. France's total population is nearly 67 million. This number is spread out across 18 administrative regions. Five of the regions are overseas.

France has a semi-presidential government. In this type of government, power is shared between a president and PM. France has a strong separation between church and state. However, the country's most practiced religion is Catholicism. The second-most-practiced religion is Islam. At roughly 7.5 percent, France has the second-highest percentage of Muslims in Europe.

France's official language is French. Some residents speak **dialects** or other languages, such as Alsatian or Basque. However, these regional differences are declining.

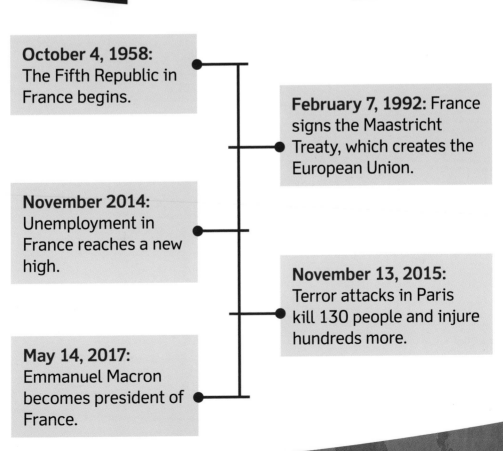

October 4, 1958: The Fifth Republic in France begins.

February 7, 1992: France signs the Maastricht Treaty, which creates the European Union.

November 2014: Unemployment in France reaches a new high.

November 13, 2015: Terror attacks in Paris kill 130 people and injure hundreds more.

May 14, 2017: Emmanuel Macron becomes president of France.

CHAPTER 4

MACRON'S RISE TO POWER

By 2012, Macron had made a name for himself as a financial advisor. His reputation earned him a job with François Hollande. Hollande was seeking his party's nomination for the 2012 presidential election. After winning the election, Hollande named Macron the deputy chief of staff at Elysée Palace. This palace is the official residence of France's president.

The Elysée Palace has 365 rooms.

In his new role, Macron pushed Hollande to make changes that would help businesses. He also helped Hollande prepare for important meetings with foreign leaders.

In summer 2014, Macron resigned from his post. But he was not done working for Hollande. Later that year, Hollande offered Macron a position in the federal government. Macron agreed and became minister of the economy.

The French economy had not seen growth for three years. As financial minister, Macron worked to change longstanding areas of the economy. This included laws about France's workweek. In France, employers must increase workers' pay when they work more than 35 hours. Macron wanted to give companies greater flexibility in deciding employees' hours. A change to the 35-hour workweek didn't happen. Some changes

#RévolutionEnMarche

Macron proposed were so unpopular that people protested.

Macron did not stay in the position for long. In April 2016, he launched his own political party, En Marche. Macron was unhappy with France's traditional parties. En Marche, or On the Move, created the possibility for new political ideas.

The movement welcomed people from different political parties. Macron wanted people with similar values to work together.

The move didn't please Hollande. Macron's new political party threatened Hollande's chances for reelection. In August 2016, Macron resigned as minister of the economy. He wanted to prepare for his presidential campaign. In November, he announced his run for the presidency. At that time, few voters knew who he was.

Macron's lack of political standing worked in his favor. Many voters were tired of the traditional political parties. They wanted change.

➤ THINK ABOUT IT

If you were a French voter, would you have voted for Macron? Why or why not?

Supporters celebrated Macron's win at the Carrousel du Louvre in Paris.

As a result, Macron did well in the first round of voting. The race revealed the changing nature of French politics. France's two major parties lost. Candidates from one of these parties had been president for decades. Instead, Macron and Le Pen remained.

As the second round approached, Hollande asked voters to support Macron. He thought Le Pen would be dangerous for France. A majority of voters listened, making Macron president.

CHAPTER 5

MACRON'S AGENDA

During the 2017 presidential campaign, France was facing major challenges. François Hollande had the lowest approval rating of any French president in history. Many citizens were not satisfied with Hollande's actions against terrorism. Hollande had also failed in adding more jobs to the economy. Macron made sure his agenda addressed these items.

Macron (right) and Hollande shake hands at the 2017 presidential inauguration.

As the former financial minister, Macron was familiar with France's economy. Improving the economy was a key point of his agenda. Macron had a five-year plan to spend 50 billion euros on energy, the environment, health care, and more. In addition, Macron created a plan to make labor laws less strict. This would give employers more control over their companies and employees. However, many workers disliked Macron's plans. They feared they would lose some of their rights.

Macron also wanted to cut business taxes. France had some of the highest business taxes in the world. Cutting them would allow businesses to spend their profits elsewhere. For example, companies could pay employees higher wages. With higher wages, employees would have more money to spend. And increased spending would boost the economy.

In September 2017, French citizens protested Macron's changes to labor laws.

Macron's opponent, Le Pen, had different plans for France's economy. She wanted France to leave the EU. Many of the EU member nations use the euro as their currency. Le Pen thought France should have its own currency. In contrast, Macron wanted France to stay in the EU and keep the euro. But he also wanted to make some changes.

As of 2017, each country in the EU had its own budget and financial minister. Macron wanted EU members to share one budget and financial minister. He thought these changes would improve **collaboration** between EU members.

Another major item in Macron's agenda was France's fight against terrorism. In November 2015, a terror attack in Paris led to 130 deaths. After the attack, France entered an official state of emergency. Eight months later, a man drove a vehicle into a crowd of people in Nice, a city in southern France. A total of 84 people died. More attacks have occurred in other areas of the nation.

During his run for president, Macron had promised to fight terrorism. He planned to collect information on terrorists through their internet use. This would allow the French government to prevent future attacks.

In December 2015, French citizens lit candles in memory of the victims of the November terrorist attack.

In his victory speech, Macron said he would unite France. He promised to serve his country with love. A week after winning the election, Macron took over as France's leader.

CHAPTER 6

TAKING ACTION AT HOME

Macron started tackling France's economic issues as soon as he took office. But fixing the French economy would not be an easy job. The government did not have much money. High government spending had caused a **deficit**.

Macron planned to cut government spending by 60 billion euros. He also planned to eliminate 120,000 government jobs. However, Macron would not force employees out of their jobs.

Macron signs his approval of bills in the presidential office.

Instead, as employees retired, the government would not refill positions.

Macron quickly began trimming the French budget. In July 2017, he slashed the country's defense budget by 850 million euros. The head of France's armed forces, Pierre de Villiers, disagreed with the cut. He quit in protest. Later that month, the government announced it would make cuts to a housing benefit. The change would affect thousands of citizens, including low-income families. Many citizens protested the proposal.

Macron also proposed tax changes that would benefit wealthy citizens. This idea frustrated many people. Macron's popularity fell from 64 percent to 54 percent. A drop of this size was rare so soon after an election. And his ratings continued to fall.

The success of Macron's economic plan is key to his career. His success also depends on his fight against terrorism. In 2017, Macron's government proposed a law to expand security. The new law would give greater power to security officials.

FALLING APPROVAL ◄

Satisfaction with Macron and Hollande in first 100 days of first term*

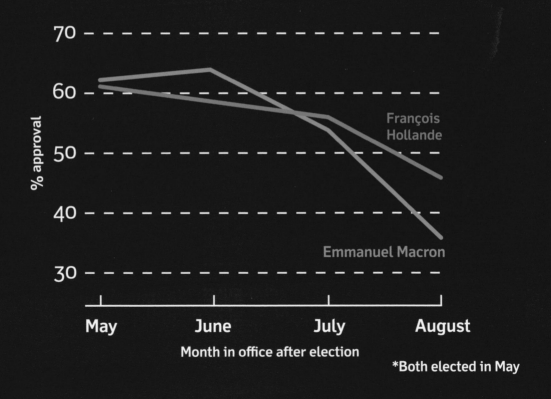

% approval

70

60

50

40

30

François Hollande

Emmanuel Macron

May   June   July   August

Month in office after election

*Both elected in May

They could close places of worship that promote **extremism**. Officials already had this power under the state of emergency. However, the law would make the power permanent. The law would also make it easier for officials to conduct searches. Many activists opposed the law. They worried it would threaten people's rights.

Some French citizens think the terrorist attacks are related to France's immigration policy. France is home to thousands of **refugees** from Africa and the Middle East. These immigrants moved to France to create better lives. However, some French citizens want a stricter immigration policy. Macron thinks differently. He wants France to help immigrants succeed in Europe.

Immigrants' trips to Europe can be dangerous. In the first half of 2017, more than 100,000 people headed to Europe through Libya. More than 2,300

▲ Refugees from Syria board a flight for France.

died in the process. Macron's actions could lower this number. In July 2017, Macron shared his plan to create immigration review centers in Libya. Immigrants looking to enter France would go to the centers to apply for French residence. Macron wanted to prevent immigrants from making the trip, only to be denied residence when they arrived.

FOCUS ON
ÉDOUARD PHILIPPE

Emmanuel Macron has an important ally in the French government. On his first day in office, Macron named Édouard Philippe as the PM. Before serving as PM, Philippe was the mayor of the French city Le Havre.

Philippe is not a member of Macron's party. He belongs to Les Républicains, a conservative party. Normally, the president selects a PM from his or her own party. But sometimes, a president's party does not win a majority in Parliament. When this happens, the president might choose a PM from another party. However, Macron's party had won a majority. He chose a PM from Les Républicains because he wanted to change politics in France.

Like Macron, Philippe attended both Sciences Po and the ENA. Philippe also studied law and worked as a lawyer. From 2007 to 2010, Philippe

Édouard Philippe waves to a crowd after the handover ceremony for the PM position.

worked at a nuclear power company. Then he decided to pursue politics instead. Philippe became a member of Parliament in 2012 and a mayor in 2014.

As PM, Philippe's job is to make Macron's agenda a reality. One of his most important tasks is working with members of the French Parliament. As a member of Les Républicains, Philippe has a better chance than Macron at appealing to members of that party. Success in this task would make Philippe extremely valuable to Macron.

CHAPTER 7

MACRON ON THE WORLD STAGE

During his first two months as president, Macron visited seven countries. He hoped to build relationships with other world leaders. His travels included trips to Germany, Morocco, and Italy. He also welcomed US President Donald Trump to France.

In July 2017, Macron announced plans to host a climate summit in December. At the summit, world leaders would discuss the Paris Agreement.

Donald Trump visited Macron in France in July 2017.

In December 2015, nearly 200 nations had signed the agreement. These nations promised to better protect the environment. But on June 1, 2017, there was an important change. Trump decided to pull the United States out of the agreement. Macron was disappointed with Trump's decision. He used Trump's campaign slogan, "Make America Great Again," against him. Macron changed the slogan to "Make Our Planet Great Again."

Macron also stepped forward in matters of the EU. In June 2016, voters in the United Kingdom voted to leave the EU. The decision became known as Brexit. The United Kingdom had one of the EU's largest economies. In 2015, it gave the third-highest amount to the EU's budget. Brexit would leave a large financial hole in the EU. Other nations have refused to pay more.

However, Macron had a plan. He hoped to use Brexit as an opportunity to draw business into France. Macron planned to attract UK companies and employees with simpler business taxes.

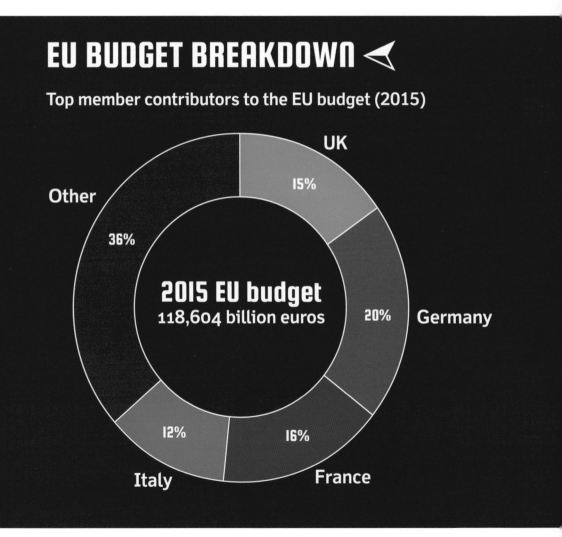

EU BUDGET BREAKDOWN ◄

Top member contributors to the EU budget (2015)

UK
15%

Other
36%

2015 EU budget
118,604 billion euros

20% Germany

12%
Italy

16%
France

Macron would also provide services to new employees looking for a place to live.

Despite Brexit, Macron offered support to the United Kingdom. On May 26, 2017, Macron met with UK Prime Minister Theresa May. Only four days earlier, there had been a terrorist attack at a concert in Manchester, England. The attack left 22 people dead and 116 injured. Macron promised to work with the United Kingdom. Together, the nations would continue fighting terrorism in Europe.

When Macron took office, he spoke of France's importance on the global stage. He explained that

➤ **THINK ABOUT IT**

Do you think it's important for world leaders to get along? Why or why not?

▲ Macron visited the British ambassador to France after the 2017 attack in Manchester, England.

the world needed France. He told French citizens that their nation must be strong and certain of itself. As president, Macron has tried to display these qualities. With a clear vision and a full agenda, he hopes to make France, Europe, and the world a better place.

FOCUS ON
EMMANUEL MACRON

Write your answers on a separate piece of paper.

1. Write a letter to a friend describing what you learned about France's 2017 presidential election.

2. Do you agree with Macron's decision to cut government jobs? Why or why not?

3. Which country's exit from the EU will give France a greater role on the world stage?

    A. Germany
    B. United Kingdom
    C. Italy

4. What might happen if Macron's plans do not improve France's economy?

    A. The EU will suffer in addition to France.
    B. The United Kingdom will stay in the EU.
    C. France will be kicked out of the EU.

Answer key on page 48.

GLOSSARY

centrist
A person who avoids extreme political positions.

collaboration
The act of working together to reach a common goal.

deficit
A situation in which more money is spent than is taken in.

dialects
Different forms of a language that are specific to a group of people.

extremism
Belief in extreme political or religious views.

foreign affairs
A country's relations and interactions with other nations.

independent
Not part of a political party.

nationalism
The belief that one's country is superior to other countries.

public policy
Government rules that affect the entire population of the country.

refugees
People forced to leave their country due to war or other dangers.

republic
A country governed by elected leaders.

terror
The use of violence to achieve a political goal.

TO LEARN MORE

BOOKS

Burgan, Michael. *The Split History of the D-Day Invasion: A Perspectives Flip Book*. North Mankato, MN: Compass Point Books, 2018.

Gogerly, Liz, and Rob Hunt. *Journey Through: France*. London: Franklin Watts, 2017.

Haywood, Karen Diane. *The French Revolution: The Power of the People*. New York: Lucent Press, 2017.

NOTE TO EDUCATORS

Visit **www.focusreaders.com** to find lesson plans, activities, links, and other resources related to this title.

INDEX

Answer Key: 1. Answers will vary; **2.** Answers will vary; **3.** B; **4.** A